FAMILY
ADVENT
DEVOTIONAL

CELEBRATE CHRIST TOGETHER

MATT & LAUREN CHANDLER

Lifeway Press®
Nashville, Tennessee

EDITORIAL TEAM

Ryane Williamson
Writer

Jennifer Siao
Production Editor

Reid Patton
Content Editor

Jon Rodda
Art Director

Joel Polk
Editorial Team Leader

Brian Daniel
Manager and Publisher, Adult Ministry

Published by Lifeway Press® • © 2021 The Village Church

ISBN 978-1-0877-1681-7 • Item 005826968

Dewey decimal classification: 263.91

Subject headings:: ADVENT / DEVOTIONAL LITERATURE / JESUS CHRIST–NATIVITY

To order additional copies of this resource, write to Lifeway Resources Customer Service; One Lifeway Plaza; Nashville, TN 37234; fax 615-251-5933; phone toll free 800-458-2772; order online at Lifeway.com; or email orderentry@lifeway.com.

Printed in the United States of America

Adult Ministry Publishing • Lifeway Resources
One Lifeway Plaza • Nashville, TN 37234

Contents

About the Authors

MATT AND LAUREN CHANDLER have been married for over 20 years—they met when Matt spoke at a camp that Lauren attended. They have had the opportunity to teach through writing, speaking, and leading worship across the world in various platforms.

Matt and Lauren have been in ministry at The Village Church in Flower Mound, Texas, for nearly 20 years. They have 3 children, Audrey, Reid and Norah.

RYANE WEINERT created the devotional content for the Advent Family Devotional. She is the Director of Resources at The Village Church. She has a passion for equipping disciples everywhere with tools to grow in their love and knowledge of God. Ryane lives in Flower Mound, Texas, with her husband, Cameron, and their son, Walt.

How to Use This Study

WHO IS THIS STUDY FOR?

This is a family devotional, but a family can look a lot of different ways. You can complete this book as parents with kids of all ages, as a couple who doesn't have children or are empty nesters, as an individual, or with a group of friends.

Family Advent Devotional: Celebrate Christ Together is 25 day, video-enhanced devotional. This book is divided into four weeks, with each week focusing on a major theme of Advent: hope, peace, love, and joy.

This devotional is meant to begin on December 1 and end on December 25. If you begin late or miss a day, try to catch up, but don't let this stop you from completing the study. If you've fallen behind, you can always simply rejoin on the appropriate day's devotional when you are able. Each day includes a Family Time devotional, conversation prompts to facilitate discussion amongst a wide variety of ages, and a prayer prompt.

DEVOTIONAL

On the first day of each week, you will watch a short video in which Matt and Lauren introduce that week's theme. On the remaining days of each week, you will read a short devotional that continues with the week's theme. You can read these on your own, with your spouse, or with the group you are completing the study with—including your kids!

To access your videos, follow these steps:
1. Open the camera app on your phone.
2. Focus on the QR Code graphic.
3. Follow the instructions that appear.

Videos may also be accessed at lifeway.com/familyadventvideos

SCRIPTURE READING

To accompany each day's devotional, there is a Scripture reading prompt. Take time to look up and read the verses, as they are typically directly connected to the daily devotionals and/or the study as a whole.

CONVERSATION PROMPTS

Each day's study includes five questions. These questions range in depth in order to facilitate conversation amongst families of all types, with members of all ages. You know your family best and can therefore determine which prompts will work for you and your group. As a general rule, the questions are written with the following audiences in mind:

PROMPT 1

For a family with a child or children between the ages of 4–7

PROMPT 2

For a family with a child or children between the ages of 8–12

PROMPT 3

For a family with teenage children

PROMPTS 4 AND 5

For adults (and teenage children)

PRAYER PROMPTS

Following each day's devotional and conversation prompts is a prayer prompt. Close your time as a group in prayer, using these short prompts to get you started. You might find these to be particularly helpful for yourself, children, or other members of your group who desire to pray but are not sure where to start.

What is Advent?

Of all the seasons in the church calendar, Advent probably feels the most familiar. Many people, regardless of faith, have used an Advent calendar—the ones with little windows to help you count down the days until Christmas. Yet, even though Advent is certainly about anticipating the coming of the Messiah, we don't seem to be very good at it, and what we generally call "Advent" looks pretty different than what the church historically has called "Advent."

Formed from a Latin word meaning "coming" or "arrival," Advent is the traditional celebration of the first advent of Jesus in humility and the anxious awaiting of His second advent in glory. The season is a time for remembering and rejoicing, watching and waiting. In American Christianity, we've got that first part down. As soon as Thanksgiving is over (and sometimes even before), we start putting up the tree and listening to our favorite Christmas songs. There's nothing wrong with doing these things, of course, but the whole point of Advent is to spend several weeks—four weeks, to be exact—preparing for Christmas instead of celebrating Christmas. It's about stepping into the shoes of the Israelites, longing and crying out for the Messiah to come. It's about reflecting on our sin and shortcomings and our need for a Savior. It's about looking around at our broken world and hoping for the second coming of Jesus. And, once we get to Christmas Day, the celebration of Jesus' birth becomes that much more spectacular and meaningful.

As we remember and enter the story of the coming of Jesus Christ, we deconstruct and deny the false stories that we find ourselves caught up in, especially those connected to our culture's concept of Christmas—individualism and consumerism. Instead, we reconstruct and embrace the true story of the gospel in our lives, specifically the focuses and themes of Advent. We recognize the weight of sin personally, corporately, and cosmically and understand why we need Jesus Christ, Immanuel, to dwell among us, restoring and reconciling creation back to the Father by the Spirit. Celebrating the Son of God coming as a gift, not to be served but to serve, we respond out of praise and gratitude, using this season to serve and to give to others.

HISTORY & TRADITIONS

The Advent season begins on the fourth Sunday before Christmas and continues up to Christmas Day, or Christmas Eve in some contexts (though for this study, we will begin on December 1 and conclude on December 25).

There are a variety of ways to celebrate the season, depending on tradition and background. Many people use an Advent calendar, typically made up of 24 "windows" containing Scriptures, stories, poems, or gifts, to count down the days until Christmas. As each window is opened and the final day draws closer, our expectation increases. This reminds us of the hopeful yet anxious waiting God's people experienced as they longed for the promised Savior to come.

Another popular tradition is marking the progression of the season through an Advent wreath made up of five candles. This symbol is borrowed from the emphasis throughout Scripture of Jesus Christ being the Light of the world (Matt. 4:16; John 1:4-9; 8:12). Each week, a new candle is lit in anticipation of Christmas Eve. The last candle, called the Christ candle, is lit on Christmas Eve to represent Jesus' first advent. Through this theme of ever-increasing light penetrating the darkness, we see a picture of the gospel.

Regardless of the tradition, Advent is a significant time in the life of the church. It's an opportunity for believers to remember God's promise to send One who would overcome sin and death forever. God promised a Savior, and He kept that promise perfectly.

WEEK 1

HOPE

DECEMBER I

HOPE

Watch

Matt and Lauren begin our study by talking about hope—one of the four main themes of the Advent season. We see hope throughout the Bible—in the Old Testament as God's people await their Savior, hope fulfilled in the New Testament when Jesus comes to earth, and hope then and now that He will one day return again.

Watch Video 1 and discuss the questions on the following page with your family or group. See page 5 for instructions on using the QR code.

Reading

Before they left the garden, God whispered a promise to Adam and Eve: "It will not always be so! I will come to rescue you! And when I do, I'm going to do battle against the snake. I'll get rid of the sin and the dark and the sadness you let in here. I'm coming back for you!" And he would. One day, God himself would come.[1]

THE JESUS STORYBOOK BIBLE[1]

Family Time

Talk about these questions with your family or group.

KIDS

1. Is there something you are really hoping for this Christmas? What is it?

2. How does the Christmas season teach us about hope? Why do Christians have hope?

TEENS AND ADULTS

3. Has there ever been a time when you placed hope in a person or circumstance and it didn't turn out like you wanted or expected? Explain the situation and why it didn't turn out like you had hoped."

4. Where we put our ultimate hope matters. Are there people, things, or circumstances you're putting your hope in right now instead of in Christ?

5. How does the hope and longing we experience as we wait for Christmas day prepare our hearts as we hope and long for Jesus' return?

Pray

Pray as a family as you begin this study that you would learn more about God over the next 25 days. Pray that as you talk about hope this week, He would make it clear to you where you may have misplaced your hope, and remind you of the hope you have because of Jesus.

DECEMBER 2

HOPE

Read Genesis 3:1-14.

When you think of the beginning of the Advent story, what do you imagine? Most of us probably picture a stable—a manger, maybe—filled with animals, a newborn Jesus, proud new parents, and lots of visitors. We think of shepherds, angels, and wise men. But, the story really begins way before that—in a garden.

You've probably heard Genesis 1 many times. God created the world—the sky, sea, land, plants, animals—and He said it was good. Then, He created people—and He said it was very good. Genesis 1:27 even tells us He created humans, male and female, in His own image! From the very beginning, people were set apart for a special relationship with God and a special role in caring for the rest of creation. At this point in the story, creation functioned in perfect order according to God's beautiful design and man walked in an unbroken relationship with God, fully known and unafraid.

But in an instant, everything changed as Adam and Eve disobeyed God's good instruction. Tempted by the snake, Eve ate the fruit from the one tree God had forbidden them to eat from. Eve offered the fruit to Adam, and he ate, as well. When they ate the fruit, they brought sin into the world. Instead of enjoying the relationship they had with God, they wanted to become just like Him. Because of that one decision to disobey Him, their fellowship with God was broken, peace was disrupted, and creation was thrown into chaos. Darkness, depravity, fear, shame, and selfishness flooded the human heart—separating people from God.

But from the very first moment we needed it, God had a rescue plan. He addresses Adam and Eve, later turns to the serpent, declaring that sin would not have the final say and that Satan would not prevail. Even amid the darkness, God spoke a word of hope, promising a Savior who would one day defeat the enemy and deliver God's people. We'll learn more about this soon.

Family Time

Talk about these questions with your family or group.

KIDS

1. Do you ever have trouble being obedient? Why can it be so hard?

2. God gave Adam and Eve everything they needed in the garden. Why do you think they chose to disobey Him?

TEENS AND ADULTS

3. How does beginning the Advent story in Genesis (instead of the New Testament) change your perspective as we enter this season? How does this impact your view of the whole story of the Bible?"

4. In what ways do we still see and feel the effects of Adam and Eve's sin, even today?

Pray

Pray that God would reveal to you areas where you have been or are currently being disobedient. Ask that these things would become clear to you and that you would move toward Him in repentance.

DECEMBER 3

HOPE

Read Genesis 3:14–19.

The brokenness of our world is inescapable—and a lot of times, it feels overwhelming. Whether you're an adult or a kid, there are lots of things—both hard and scary things—happening in our world that you've heard about. Though we hate seeing and hearing about these things, we know why they exist. Remember what we read yesterday? Sin entered into the world in Genesis 3, and it wasn't going away anytime soon.

The effects of sin aren't just big, global things—they're personal, too. With the arrival of sin came sickness, death, sadness, fear—all of the things most of us wish we could avoid. And like we saw in today's reading, it also meant that things like having children and even our work would be harder than we'd like them to be. With childbirth comes pain, with our jobs or school come boredom, anxiety, and exhaustion, and even our relationships with friends and family often prove difficult. All of these things have been affected by the fall.

But the season of Advent breaks into our broken world and turns our hearts toward a better reality—that the present darkness we so often feel has been defeated in Jesus Christ. Advent turns us—the body of Christ—away from despair and toward hope. In the same verses we read today that show us how and why sin seems to touch every aspect of our lives, we also see that we have cause for great hope. Even when Adam and Eve disobeyed God, He made them a promise—a Savior is coming. God allowed sin to enter the world, but He always had a plan to rescue His children.

When the weight of sin in our world feels overwhelming, let us be reminded that we are a people whose hearts should be broken by the darkness and brokenness that surrounds us, but we are not without hope.

Family Time

Talk about these questions with your family or group.

KIDS

1. What are some things that make you feel scared? What makes you feel happy?

2. What do you do when you feel scared? Who do you turn to? Why?

TEENS AND ADULTS

3. How do you see and feel the effects of sin in the world today? Think both big picture and personally.

4. Consider one specific thing in your life that's being affected by your sin and brokenness (a job, relationship, etc.). How would true hope in Christ change that situation or relationship?

5. Christians have great hope despite the pain and brokenness of the world. Do you ever struggle to truly believe this? What makes believing this hard?

Pray

Pray that your heart would break for the sin and brokenness we see in the world. Pray that you would take the effects of sin seriously and truly believe in the greater hope we, as Christians, have in Jesus Christ.

DECEMBER 4

HOPE

Read Genesis 3:20-24.

Yesterday we read that in Genesis 3:15 that God said, "I will put enmity between you and the woman, and between your offspring and her offspring; he shall bruise your head, and you shall bruise his heel." It might not seem obvious the first (or second or third) time that you read it, but in this passage—from the moment sin entered the world—God is promising to send humanity a Rescuer. At that point, God's people didn't know who they were waiting for or even how that person would save them, but throughout the Old Testament, God spoke to His people about this promise and gave them things to watch for as they awaited the Savior's arrival.

God revealed that the Messiah would be born in the line of David (Isa. 9:6-7), of the tribe of Judah (Gen. 49:10), and in the town of Bethlehem (Mic. 5:2). He would be a man of sorrows—crushed, despised, and rejected—justifying many through what He suffered (Isa. 53). The promised Deliverer would be a light overcoming darkness (Isa. 9:2), a preacher of good news to the poor (Isa. 61:1), and One walking in the power of the Spirit (Isa. 42:1). There were hints and shadows of Him everywhere.

God also reminded His people not to lose heart as they waited for the Savior to come—He didn't fulfill His promise right away. His people waited a long time. They spoke of the promised Rescuer from generation to generation, enduring cycles of war, rebellion, captivity, and restoration. They watched and waited—anxiously and expectantly—for God's faithfulness. Though they had to wait a long time to see this promise fulfilled, they had hope. They knew that God always keeps His promises. And so too we wait for Him to come again.

Family Time

Talk about these questions with your family or group.

KIDS

1. Have you ever gone on a scavenger hunt? How did it feel only having little hints and clues about how the scavenger hunt would end? What was fun about that and what was frustrating or hard?

2. Can you think of a time when you needed help with something? Who did you ask for help?

TEENS AND ADULTS

3. What is God promising His people in Genesis 3:15? Why is this important to the whole story of the Bible?

4. If God's plan was always to rescue His people from sin, why do you think He allowed sin to enter the world in the first place?

5. From Genesis to Revelation we see that God always keeps His promises. Do you believe this to be true for your life? What makes it hard to believe?

Pray

Pray that you would be aware of the sin in your life in such a way that you see your need for Jesus, our Rescuer. Pray that throughout this Advent season and beyond, you would truly believe God keeps all of His promises, and that just like He promised a Savior once, He has promised the Savior will come again.

DECEMBER 5

HOPE

Read Exodus 3:7-22.

We have lost our ability to wait well—or perhaps at all. With services like same-day shipping, mobile food ordering, streaming services, and even grocery delivery, we can have anything we need as soon as we want it. As technology develops and our demand for convenience grows, many of us seem to have lost a discipline we see throughout Scripture—the art of waiting. Yesterday, we talked about the hints throughout the Bible about who God's people were waiting for, but what might it have been like and felt like to wait all that time?

Consider Moses and the story of the Exodus. For generations, God's people suffered hardship under the rule of Pharaoh, and apart from the provision and power of God, they were helpless to save themselves. So the Israelites—sometimes patiently and other times with deep frustration—waited for their rescuer, until (finally), God sent Moses to deliver them from slavery.

In the same way God's people were made to wait for their deliverance from Egypt, God didn't send Jesus to save His people right away. In fact, He waited thousands of years to send the promised Rescuer, sometimes leaving them wondering if He had forgotten them altogether. But God continued to whisper it over and over again as His children waited, knowing that one day, when no one was expecting it, Jesus—their Rescuer and ours—would come.

Though pictures of faithful waiting and of promises fulfilled throughout the Bible should fill us with great hope, we still struggle to wait well. But Advent calls us out of our natural state of impatience and toward unhurried waiting. Like we read in today's Scripture—God promised to raise someone up who would establish His forever Kingdom. We know that the promises one is Jesus, and we know that He has come and that He will come again. But for now, full of hope and longing, we wait.

Family Time

Talk about these questions with your family or group.

KIDS

1. Think about the last time you had to wait for something you were really excited about. Was it hard or is it easy to wait?

2. Why is waiting so hard?

TEENS AND ADULTS

3. Imagine you were an Israelite in Egypt, waiting to be rescued from slavery and hardship. "Would it have been hard to trust God as you waited? What would you have done to keep your hopes up as you waited and endured hardships?

4. How have you let convenience and impatience rule your life? What habits could you consider changing in order for you to practice the art of patience and waiting?

5. Surely the Israelites doubted that God would keep His promises. In what ways do you sometimes struggle with doubt?

Pray

Pray for courage to consider the ways you have chosen convenience
over patience and hope in God's plans and timing. Pray that
in your moments of doubt, God would help your unbelief.

DECEMBER 6

HOPE

Read Mark 13:32-37.

It happens every year—what we expect to be a slower-paced summer flies by, and before we know it, it's Labor Day weekend. Fireworks give way to football, then pumpkins to pilgrims. Now, it's all we can do to finish our Christmas shopping and get our yuletide greetings in the mail before the "guaranteed delivery by Christmas" date. And the reality is, if left unchecked, we'll be right here again this time next year wondering, "Where did the time go?" We get busy with our day-to-day lives, lulling ourselves into a trance—just trying to make it through the year, letting the important things sneak up on us or forgetting them altogether.

But the Advent season calls us from this daze—from our slumber. It bursts into our passivity and calls us to "stay awake." We've been talking all week about the hope we have because of Jesus' promise to return, and His words from Mark 13:32-37 are a stunning reminder that He will come again. Our Master has departed on a journey, but He's left us with work to do while He's away. And the work we're called into cannot be put off until later because Jesus' second advent will come at a day and hour that only the Father knows.

It's so easy to get lulled into slumber by the turning of time, passing by at what seems to be an ever-increasing pace. But this sleepy apathy while we wait is not the life we've been called to live. The Great Commission in Matthew 28—Jesus' instruction to His disciples that's been passed down to us—says, "Go therefore and make disciples of all nations, baptizing them in the name of the Father and of the Son and of the Holy Spirit... And behold, I am with you always, to the end of the age."

Advent reminds us that we are a commissioned people, granted stewardship of the gospel message. We have the privilege of heralding this message day by day, season by season, year by year, eagerly anticipating the return of Christ. Our Master is away, but He's coming again.

Family Time

Talk about these questions with your family or group.

KIDS

1. What was your favorite part of this year? Are there any memories that stand out?

2. Did this year feel like it went by quickly or slowly? Why do you think it felt the way it did?

TEENS AND ADULTS

3. What do you think it means when the Bible says to "stay awake" for the return of Jesus? How can you practice staying awake for His return in your life?"

4. In what ways do you feel yourself "falling asleep"? How can you shift from passivity to active obedience and participation in God's plans?

5. The Great Commission calls all of us to tell others about Jesus and make disciples. Do you feel comfortable telling others about Jesus and your faith? What might be stopping you?

Pray

Pray that you would awaken from the sleepy daze of everyday life and enter into active participation in God's story. Pray for boldness to share the good news of the gospel with others as you eagerly await Jesus' return.

DECEMBER 7

HOPE

Read Isaiah 9:1-7.

So far this week, we've learned that sin has separated us from God, and we feel those effects globally, but also personally—in our relationships, jobs, school—everywhere! But God promised to send a Rescuer to save us from our sin—and He did. Jesus, God the Son, came to earth, died for our sins, rose from the grave, and now He is ruling and reigning at the right hand of God the Father until He comes again. Because of this, we have great hope and confidence—God keeps His promises and Jesus will come back one day for His people.

Despite knowing these things, we are easily distracted from them. We don't spend much time recentering our hearts around and intentionally meditating on the hope of Jesus most of the year. We float adrift, untethered from this truth, and what is the result? Misplaced hope and confidence—trusting in things like friends, work, or our sports teams instead of Jesus.

Maybe you've heard sermons or had conversations about where you place your hope and why we struggle to make Jesus the answer to that question. It might feel like a tired question, but there's a reason we ask it so often. We need to be constantly reminded of and pulled back toward Jesus and the hope we have in Him. Advent provides space and time to do that after we've felt ourselves wandering throughout the year. Our hearts and minds are recaptured by the story and beauty of Jesus, making it clearer than ever that when we place our hope in anything other than Him, we will certainly be let down.

Isaiah reminds us why we can so confidently place our hope in Him. The prophet wrote "the government shall be upon his shoulder" (v. 6), "[of his] peace there will be no end" (v. 7), and "on the throne of David and over his kingdom, to establish it and uphold it with justice and with righteousness from this time forth and forevermore" (v. 7). What more could we ask for? What better place could there be for our hope?

Family Time

Talk about these questions with your family or group.

KIDS

1. What is one thing you've learned this week about Jesus, the Bible, or hope?

2. What do you spend most of your time thinking about? What are some ways you could practice thinking more about Jesus and the hope we have because of Him?

TEENS AND ADULTS

3. Why is placing our hope in anyone or anything other than God ultimately going to let us down?

4. How does true hope in Jesus change the way you think about your life? How might it affect your friendships, marriage, job, school, an so forth?

5. How does true hope in Jesus change the way you see the world?

Pray

Pray that your thoughts would constantly be pulled back to the beauty and hope of Jesus. Pray that God would reveal places in your life where you have misplaced your hope instead of putting it in Him.

ADVENT

WEEK 2

PEACE

DECEMBER 8

PEACE

Watch

Watch this week's video with your family or group as Matt and Lauren talk about peace—the theme for our second week of Advent. In a season that tends to bring chaos and anxiety, we'll begin to see how the story of Jesus offers overwhelming peace for those who believe in Him.

Watch Video 2 and discuss the questions on the following page with your family or group. See page 5 for instructions on using the QR code.

Scripture

Come to me, all who labor and are heavy laden, and I will give you rest. Take my yoke upon you, and learn from me, for I am gentle and lowly in heart, and you will find rest for your souls. For my yoke is easy, and my burden is light.

MATTHEW 11:28–30

Family Time

Talk about these questions with your family or group.

KIDS

1. Does Christmastime feel busy or calm? What fun things do you and your family have planned for the next few weeks?

2. Do you know what peace means? What's a time you can remember that was really peaceful?

TEENS AND ADULTS

3. Share about a time when your life wasn't peaceful. Where did you seek comfort?

4. Why does the Advent season bring peace to those who believe in Jesus?

5. What areas of your life do you currently see as chaotic and stressful? How could you step away from that chaos and into the peace of God?

Pray

Pray that, as a family, you would learn about, talk about, and enjoy the peace of Jesus this week and all throughout the Advent season. Pray that throughout this week, God would help you slow down and focus on Him.

DECEMBER 9

PEACE

Read Luke 1:26–38.

Mary. A key player in the story of Advent and the first coming of Christ. Today, we read Luke's retelling of the day she found out that she—a virgin—would give birth to the King and Son of the Most High. She was scared—and how could she not have been? Pause for just a moment to imagine her situation. What would you have felt? Excitement? Joy? Maybe, but more likely you would feel shocked, confused, and frightened. Yet, the angel, Gabriel, tells her not to be afraid. Why? Because though the announcement brings momentary fear, it ultimately brings a declaration of peace that Mary—or anyone else—had never heard before. After so many years, Gabriel brought news of the long-awaited Savior.

As hard as it might have been for Mary to wrap her mind around what she had just heard, that event was just the beginning. The angel left, and the reality of the news sank in. The incredible promise spoken by Gabriel faded into the reality of being a young, not-yet-married woman who had to answer to her future husband, her family, and all those she encountered about the nature of her pregnancy.

Luke tells us that Mary stayed with Elizabeth for three months, but we aren't told much else about what her pregnancy was like. As with any pregnancy, there were likely difficult days and happy days. Regardless, her pregnancy must have been marked by a sense of expectancy. Not just because she was anticipating the arrival of the Son of God, but because she was expecting.

As she waited for His arrival, Mary surely wrestled with doubt and fear, but she was likely comforted by the words of Gabriel. "Do not be afraid," he said. In her waiting, Mary got a glimpse of a new kind of peace that would soon come to earth—brought about by her very own Son who, right now, was just a baby in her womb. We too, sit in this peace—knowing He has come before and He will one day come again.

Family Time

Talk about these questions with your family or group.

KIDS

1. Can you remember a time when you heard a very surprising news? How did you respond?

2. How do you think Mary felt when Gabriel came to give her the news that she would have a baby?

TEENS AND ADULTS

3. What makes you afraid? What helps you when you are afraid? How does Jesus help ease your fears?

4. Think about when you or a friend or family member were pregnant. How did a sense of expectancy mark the pregnancy? Did attitudes and expectations change throughout? How does this inform the way you think about expecting Christ's return?

5. Though she was scared, Mary showed incredible openness to God's plans for her when she received the angel's news. In what areas might God be calling you to deeper faith and openness to His will?

Pray

Pray that God would reveal areas of your life where you may be operating out of fear, and that you would begin to trust Him more and more with those things. Pray that, where you may be holding tightly to plans of your own, you would walk in deeper faith and openness to His will.

DECEMBER 10

PEACE

Read Isaiah 7:14.

Mary waited, like any expectant mother, for her baby to be born. Perhaps those weeks and months dragged on, or maybe they flew by—we can't know. But we do know that though Mary's waiting may have, at times, felt long, it was nothing compared to how long her people, the Israelites, had been waiting for this moment.

Remember what we read about last week in Genesis? God promised a Savior from the earliest days. The Israelites had waited thousands of years, and finally, without most of them even knowing it had happened, God fulfilled His promise. Jesus had arrived. God had given His people hints about their coming King—He would come from Bethlehem and be a ruler who brought great peace. Naturally, many expected a soldier. Others, a politician. But no one expected this—a baby, born in a *stable*. Jesus, the King of heaven, left His perfect home in heaven to be born as a baby.

But everything happened exactly as God planned and promised. We've already seen prophecies throughout the Old Testament of the promised Savior, but the one we read today in Isaiah 7 says, "Therefore the Lord himself will give you a sign. Behold, the virgin shall conceive and bear a son, and shall call his name Immanuel."

Immanuel simply means this: "God with us." We see this idea—God with us—throughout the Bible. God was with Adam and Eve in the garden. He was with His people as they wandered through the desert, in Egypt, and in exile. But now Immanuel takes a whole new form—Jesus became *God with us*. Fully God and fully man, He came to dwell with His people on the earth. And though now He is not physically here, He is with us still today as we wait for His return. After His life, death, and resurrection, He sent us the Holy Spirit. For believers in Christ, the Holy Spirit is God with us, each and every day. As we continue this Advent season, let that bring unfathomable peace. *God is with us, even now.*

Family Time

Talk about these questions with your family or group.

KIDS

1. What do you think it was like the day you were born?

2. Can you remember what "Immanuel" means? How does knowing that God is with us give us peace?

TEENS AND ADULTS

3. Why do you think Jesus was born as a baby in a stable, and not as a baby born into a fancy family, or as a king like we usually think of Him?

4. Think through the story of Scripture. List some of the different ways that we see "God with us" throughout the Bible.

5. Do you always feel God's presence with you? Why is it sometimes easier to feel than others? Are there habits and practices you can cultivate to remind yourself that, through the Holy Spirit, God is with you?

Pray

Pray that you would rightly celebrate over the next couple of weeks the coming of our Savior King! Pray that throughout the rest of the Advent season and beyond, you would feel God's nearness as you encounter Him through Scripture, prayer, and the people around you.

DECEMBER 11

PEACE

Read Luke 2:8–12.

Today's Scripture brought what is likely another familiar story—the story of the shepherds. We start here: the shepherds were watching their flock at night, but the stillness and calm of the darkness was interrupted by an angel of the Lord coming to tell them of Jesus' birth. God's glory shined brightly, and the shepherds were surprised, terrified, and in awe as they heard the angel say to them, "Fear not."

You and I typically jump ahead to the next part of the story—that they made their way to see the baby boy. But like we did with Mary's story, let's really consider this scene. Think about that night—the sky opening up and the glory of the Lord shining bright around these shepherds. Their hearts trembled at the angel who said to them, "Fear not, for behold, I bring you good news of great joy that will be for all the people. For unto you is born this day in the city of David a Savior, who is Christ the Lord."

And if the presence of one angel was not enough to make the point for these shepherds, many more angels appeared saying, "Glory to God in the highest, and on earth peace among those with whom he is pleased!" Just like Gabriel brought news of peace to Mary, this host of angels promised peace on earth through the newly-born King.

Like the angels burst into the darkness, so too has light exposed the darkness of our own hearts! In Jesus we have a Rescuer. Without Him we are, at best, a disappointing version of who we wish to be. But He has come to bring light—and peace—to the darkest places of our hearts. So our hearts still tremble now, not with fear at His appearing, but in awe of the overwhelming peace we have, because He has come to save us.

Family Time

Talk about these questions with your family or group.

KIDS

1. What is a shepherd? What is their job? Do you think people thought they were important or not important?

2. Do you think the shepherds would have expected to be some of the first people to hear that Jesus, the King, had been born? Why or why not?

TEENS AND ADULTS

3. Why is it important that the shepherds actually went to see Jesus after they heard about His birth from the angels?

4. How do you think they reacted to this news? Do you think they realized the angels were finally bringing news of the promised Savior they'd been waiting for for hundreds of years?

5. Are there areas of darkness in your life that need to be exposed by the light? Consider your answer and share if you are comfortable. If not, spend some time praying this week for courage to step into the light.

Pray

Pray that God would help you understand the magnitude and importance of the news the shepherds received that night. Pray that you, too, would be so excited by Jesus that you take action by telling the good news of His birth! Lastly, pray that where you are living in darkness and sin, that you would have the courage to step into the light.

DECEMBER 12

PEACE

Read Ephesians 2:14-16.

Prince of peace is a term you've probably heard used often around this time of year. Maybe you're familiar with it because of Isaiah 9:6 (which we read last week). Or perhaps you've heard it in as a lyric in one of your favorite Christmas songs, like "Hark! The Herald Angels Sing." But have you ever really stopped to consider what this term, this title for Jesus, really means? What is the role of the "Prince of Peace"?

Today's reading told us that Jesus "himself is our peace" (v. 14). It also says that He would "create in himself one new man in the place of two, so making peace," and that He would "reconcile us both to God in one body through the cross, thereby killing the hostility" (vv. 15–16). We're getting closer, but you probably still have some questions about what, exactly, this means.

Though Christmas is the time where we celebrate the birth of Jesus, it's important we don't forget all that He came to earth to do after that moment. Jesus had a job to do—we've said it many times—He came to be our Savior. He came as a baby, yes, but then He lived a perfect life, died for our sins, rose from the dead, and went back to heaven. And in His death He did just what these verses in Ephesians explain: He tore down the dividing wall of hostility between God and people. He died for our sins so that we would be fully, freely, and forever forgiven—so that we could be reconciled to God and enjoy all that there is in relationship with Him.

This "Prince" didn't come to live a life of luxury or ease. He wasn't waiting in line, hoping He'd one day get to take His place on the throne. He knew His job and He knew how it would end. He came with a mission—a battle—in mind, and He accomplished it. Through His death and resurrection, He waged war against sin and He was victorious. That is our Prince of peace.

Family Time

Talk about these questions with your family or group.

KIDS

1. Who are some examples of a prince or princess that you know of? What do you think it would be like to be a prince or princess?

2. If you were a prince or princess, what is one rule you'd like to make for your kingdom?

TEENS AND ADULTS

3. When was a time when you were in charge of something? Why is it difficult to be in charge?

4. How does Jesus accomplish His role as the Prince of peace? Why does His job as a peace-bringer have to involve waging war?

5. Are there areas of your life where you need to start waging war on sin? How does knowing Jesus has already defeated those things help you have the courage to get serious about fighting sin?

Pray

Thank God that He sent His Son, Jesus, to wage war on sin and be our Prince of peace. Pray for the courage to bring your own sin into light and community so that you can fight it with God's help.

DECEMBER 13

PEACE

Read Luke 2:13-14.

You know that game you used to play as a kid (or still play on occasion now) where you imagine what you would say if a genie appeared granting you three wishes? Perhaps you wanted a certain toy or to go on a trip somewhere far away. But do you remember one of the most common wishes? Maybe we meant it or maybe we felt like we had to say it—but most of us, at some point, wished for world peace.

We were asking for our version of peace on earth—no more fighting, sadness, sickness, or death. All would be right in our eyes, if only peace came to earth. But didn't we talk just yesterday about how peace did come through Jesus' birth? Yet we look around and see that our world is still full of hard and scary things.

Despite what we read in today's Scripture reading, Jesus' birth and work on earth didn't bring peace in the way that we might imagine. Like we learned yesterday, He brought peace between people and God, and through that reconciliation, He also made a way for peace between people. But as long as there is sin in the world— and there will be until Jesus returns—we won't see peace (the kind we imagine) over all the earth. We will continue to witness devastating and frightening things.

So how do we respond when we look around at the state of the world? One thing we can do is lament—we can be honest, expressing our sadness and even anger to God over the state of the world. Christmas isn't often the time where we focus on lament, but it's a good practice nonetheless. Because of Jesus, we have access to God, through the Spirit. We can pour out our feelings to Him, knowing that He is listening and compassionate when His children come to Him.

A genie will never grant our wishes for world peace, but we have something so much better. We have Jesus, who has made peace between us and God, and we have the assured hope that He will one day return again to make all things right in the world.

Family Time

Talk about these questions with your family or group.

KIDS

1. If you got to make three wishes, what would they be? What is the difference between making a wish and praying to God?

2. What do you think a peaceful world would look like?

TEENS AND ADULTS

3. Do you ever ask God for things like He's a genie waiting to grant your wishes? Why is this dangerous?

4. Where can you be a messenger of God's peace? Think about work, school, your relationships, and so forth.

5. Are there things in your life or the world that you need to lament? Where do you see brokenness and pain, but feel hesitant to talk to God about it?

Pray

Pray that God would open your eyes to the things in the world that break His heart. Pray for space and time to honestly lament all that is not right in the world. Pray that, as you lament, you would not forget the deeply-seeded peace we have through Jesus Christ, and that we would wait expectantly for Him to return and make all things right.

DECEMBER 14

PEACE

Read Colossians 3:12-17.

Think back to the beginning of this week and the video you watched—we talked about the chaos and craziness of this time of year. Are you feeling it yet? There are presents to wrap, parties to attend, and meals to prepare. Maybe you feel distracted throughout the day, or you're waking up at odd hours of the night to make and review the lists in your head over and over again. It doesn't feel possible to do it all, and there's a whole slew of people who you fear you'll disappoint if you fail. Are you feeling that Christmas spirit yet?

Well, just like the effects of sin are not only global but also personal, so, too, are the effects of peace. We long for the day when Christ returns to restore perfect peace to the world, but we shouldn't forget what this means for each of us, individually—in the big picture of our lives, yes, but also in the little, stressful moments of each day. And right now, in what can be a crazy season, we're not meant to feel guilt or shame when we feel overwhelmed. Instead, we should see these moments and feelings of it all just being "too much" as an invitation to find rest.

Perfect peace has come through Jesus Christ, and we have free access to it. So when we feel pressure coming from all sides to enter into and even celebrate chaos, we can pause and remember everything we've talked about this week—our God is the God of true, lasting peace in this moment, this season, and always. We can take time to be still, to pray, and to remember all that is true and beautiful about Him.

We are called to share the good news of Jesus. Consider your friends, family, neighbors, coworkers, and teammates. We have the opportunity to connect this seasonal celebration with the Prince of peace. So throughout Advent and beyond, slow down and consider where you need to step away from chaos and into the peace of Jesus. Then, look up and look around, be bold, and begin to share the gospel of peace to all the earth, beginning first with those right in front of you.

Family Time

Talk about these questions with your family or group.

KIDS

1. What is one thing you learned this week about Jesus, the Bible, or peace?

2. Now that we've learned about the peace that Jesus brings, does the word "peace" mean something different to you?

TEENS AND ADULTS

3. How is biblical peace different from worldly peace (which means something more like "relaxing")?

4. Are there people around you who need the peace of Jesus? Think of at least one person who needs to hear this news and one step you can take toward sharing it with them.

5. Our culture is quick to celebrate busyness and chaos. How have you played into this? Where in your life do you need to step out of chaos and into peace?

Pray

Thank God that He has given us an alternative to chaos and stress through the peace of Christ. Pray that He would open your eyes to those around you who don't know this type of peace, and that you would be courageous to share it with them this Advent season.

ADVENT

WEEK 3

LOVE

DECEMBER 15

LOVE

Watch

In this week's video, Matt and Lauren talk about love. "Love" is a word we often use loosely, but this week we'll consider what biblical love really means and how it might change the way we approach this Advent season.

Watch Video 3 and discuss the questions on the following page with your family or group. See page 5 for instructions on using the QR code.

Scripture

For God so loved the world, that he gave his only Son, that whoever believes in him should not perish but have eternal life. For God did not send his Son into the world to condemn the world, but in order that the world might be saved through him.

JOHN 3:16-17

Family Time

Talk about these questions with your family or group.

KIDS

1. What do you think love means?

2. How does Jesus being born as a baby show us God's love?

TEENS AND ADULTS

3. Do you ever struggle with guilt that you "haven't loved God enough"? What good news do we have, despite this sometimes being true?

4. How can we remind our hearts and minds of the love of God during this Advent season?

5. Do you ever feel like you are unworthy to receive the love of God? Why? What can you do to remind yourself of the truth about His love for you?

Pray

Pray that God would prepare your heart and mind to learn about love this week. Pray that you would really begin to understand the difference between the worldly definition of love and the biblical definition of love. Thank God for loving you and for sending His Son into the world for you.

DECEMBER 16

LOVE

Read 1 John 4:7–9.

As we begin this week that is all about *love*, let's start with a definition. One source says that to love someone or something is to "like or enjoy [it] very much." [2] If that's true, then it's easy to see why we so often use this word the way we do. If you "like or enjoy" playing with friends, watching sports, baking, or going on long runs, according to this definition, you actually love those things.

The Bible provides a very different and more robust picture of "love." In the New International Version of the Bible, the word is used 425 times in the Old Testament and 261 times in the New. The New Testament, originally written in Greek, uses multiple words for love, depending on the author's context. C.S. Lewis often focused on the "four loves"[3]:

STORGE
familial love

PHILOS
love that describes deep friendship

EROS
physical or romantic love

AGAPE
selfless, unconditional love[2]

The Bible doesn't just talk about feelings of love, but the commandment to love. In Matthew 22, Jesus tells us that the greatest commandment of any is to "love the Lord your God." The second? To love our neighbors.

So what does this have to do with Advent? Jesus' birth brought a new kind of love. In fact, He didn't just bring love, He is love. As we continue learning about the love of God made visible through the birth and life of His only Son, remember this: "love" was never meant to be a watered-down, worn out word used to describe any and everything. True love—biblical love—is powerful and significant, and we understand it best by turning and looking to Jesus.

Family Time

Talk about these questions with your family or group.

KIDS

1. What are some ways that we can love God with our words and actions?

2. What or who are we supposed to love most? Is it okay to love things besides God?

TEENS AND ADULTS

3. What are other examples or stories about love you've learned about from the Bible? Share those with each other.

4. How is our love for God supposed to be different from our love for people or things?

5. What or who do you love more than God right now? Why is it easier to love those things more than God?

Pray

Thank God that He loves you. Pray that you would see clearly the things in your life that you love more than Him, and that as you learn more about biblical love this week, you would begin to understand and desire it more than worldly love.

DECEMBER 17

LOVE

Read 1 John 4:10-12.

Christmastime is a time for love—to show love to family, friends, and neighbors. With all the festivities surrounding us, this should be easy, right? For some of us, it may be. But for others, this holiday is less of an easy demonstration of love, and more a test of it. Perhaps you know you'll spend the day with that family member who, simply put, just really drives you crazy. Maybe you'll be spending the holidays alone despite wanting to show love to others (or wanting desperately to receive it). Or for many, this is your first Christmas without someone you love dearly.

Whether you are excited about the coming celebration of Jesus' birth or dreading the feelings it may stir up inside of you, there is a shared need among us all. No matter where we find ourselves on this spectrum, the call to love at Christmastime (and all the time) highlights our dependence on God. In the verses we read today, John says, "Beloved, if God so loved us, we also ought to love one another."

God's love for us moved far beyond "feelings" and into decisive action. He loved us so much that He sent Jesus to be born, to live, and to die for our sins. In response, we ought to offer a similar response to those around us. No sacrifice of our time or energy could ever compare to the sacrifice of Christ, but in this season we have a unique opportunity to imitate Him. See, love is not simply how we feel. Love for others, like the love of Jesus, is made manifest in our actions.

So, no matter how you may "feel"—whether you find yourself in the "holiday spirit" or like each day of this time of year is another hurdle for you to clear—Advent ought to be a welcome reminder of your complete dependence on God and to demonstrate His love. Every day of this season provides a reminder that apart from God, we cannot truly know love, and without Him, we cannot rightly give it.

Family Time

Talk about these questions with your family or group.

KIDS

1. What do you love about Christmas?

2. What are some ways you can show the people around you that you love them?

TEENS AND ADULTS

3. This Christmas, does showing love to others feel easy or challenging? Share what might be making this year, in particular, a hard year for you to celebrate. Or, how has it been easy to love others this Christmas?"

4. Is there someone in your life who is hard to love? What does your struggle to love them reveal about you? What can you do to take steps toward showing them the tangible love of God?

5. Do you tend to get stuck thinking of love as just a feeling? How can you shift love from being a thought in your head or feeling in your heart to tangible actions with your hands?

Pray

Pray that God would comfort you if this Christmas season is highlighting loneliness, difficult relationships, or the loss of a loved one. Pray that God would open your eyes to see others who are hurting, and in complete dependence on Him, you would take steps toward demonstrating His love to those around you.

DECEMBER 18

LOVE

Read 1 John 4:13–19.

What is the greatest picture of love you've ever seen? Is it the love you've witnessed between your parents? Friends? The way you love your children? Maybe what came to mind first wasn't anyone you actually know, but an iconic couple from a show or movie. Pause for a second and think about what made that love so special—what makes it stand out and why is it unique? All of these love stories, whether they are real or fictional, have flaws. No matter how perfect they may seem, we know that they are not.

There is only one story in the history of the world that paints a picture for us of perfect love. Does that sound cliché, or perhaps even cheesy to you? That's understandable—but the truth remains the same. And as we find ourselves in the middle of Advent, we also find ourselves in the middle of this great story.

As we've talked about during the last couple of weeks, God spent years setting the stage for this love to be revealed in its fullest form, and as we approach Christmas Day, we near closer and closer to the celebration of the day God's love was, at last, made manifest on earth through Jesus Christ. Earlier this week, we read 1 John 4:9, which says, "In this the love of God was made manifest among us, that God sent his only Son into the world, so that we might live through him."

We celebrate during Advent that we have been given the greatest love story of all time as God's love for us is revealed through the sending of His Son. We see love made visible in the coming of Christ. So now what do we do? "We love because he first loved us" (1 John 4:19). God initiated this love—He moved toward us through the sending of Jesus. So now, we respond by receiving the good news of the coming of Christ as heaven's "I love you." Then, we tell Him that we love Him, too—through our words, our actions, and our worship, especially now as we prepare to celebrate the birth of Jesus—the day perfect love took human form.

Family Time

Talk about these questions with your family or group.

KIDS

1. Who loves us perfectly? How is that different from other people who love us?

2. Who came to mind when you thought about a picture of love?

TEENS AND ADULTS

3. Think about the people you love the most. What makes those relationships fun and beautiful? What makes them challenging?

4. God moves toward us in love despite our sins and failures. Do you ever struggle to believe this? Why or why not?

5. How might your days look different if you truly believed you were a recipient of the love of God? What are some ways you can respond to Him in love?

Pray

Thank God for moving toward us in love, despite our sin and failures, as He sent His Son to dwell among us on the earth. Pray for understanding to receive this unique type of love, and that you would respond with worship and adoration.

DECEMBER 19

LOVE

Read Hebrews 12:4-11.

What does it mean that "God is love"? Think, for a moment, about your parents or another significant adult in your life. Does the unconditional love of a parent equate to a times of happiness, fun, and ease? Sometimes, it does. But the love of a parent also requires discipline and hard conversations. The more we love someone, the more we feel inclined to feel angry, scared, or heartbroken on their behalf. You probably feel protective and defensive of those you love the most, willing to keep them safe by any means necessary.

This type of love is powerful, yet it is just a shadow of God's love for His children. We are quick to meditate on and talk about the "easy" parts of His love for us—that it is unconditional and everlasting, and that it is more profound than any earthly love we will ever experience. We're less comfortable, though, with the reality that His discipline and wrath are also present in this love.

God is serious about the flourishing of His people, and with that, He is serious about sin. God disciplines His children because He loves them. Does a loving parent let their children sit in the things that will cause them pain and hardship? No, through loving rebuke, they call them out of those things and into something better—even when that requires discipline.

So why are we talking about this during Advent and not a few months from now during Lent—the season in which we spend time meditating on our sin and need for a Savior? Because when we say that God—the Father, Son, and Spirit—is love, and when we sing that "love came down at Christmas," it's important that we know what we are saying. The good news of this Advent season is that Jesus came to save sinners—because He loves sinners. He was born so that He could live a perfect life, die the death we deserved, defeat sin and death, and then send the Holy Spirit to help us, all these years later, to walk in these truths. That is a birthday and a love worth celebrating.

Family Time

Talk about these questions with your family or group.

KIDS

1. How do you know that your family loves you?

2. When you get in trouble, does that feel like "love" to you? Why or why not?

TEENS AND ADULTS

3. Think of a time where you were disciplined but you can now see the ways in which that was an act of love. Did you deserve to be disciplined? In that moment, did you deserve the love you received?

4. Are there situations or relationships in your life where you have chosen ease over difficult but necessary conversations? How could the latter be a better demonstration of love?

5. In what ways is it hard for you to reconcile that our God is compassionate and kind, yet also capable of wrath? Can you recall any stories from the Bible that help encourage us that this righteous anger is often, actually, a good thing?

Pray

Thank God that He is love, and pray that He would help you to understand more deeply what this truly means. Pray that you would begin to not fear His wrath and discipline, but that you would begin to see it for what it truly is—a loving display of His desire for the flourishing of His children.

DECEMBER 20

LOVE

Read Matthew 5:44-45.

We've been learning about what it means that perfect love came to earth through the birth of Christ. This single event—the reason we enjoy this Advent season and Christmas day—changed the course of history, but it should also change us personally. Jesus has shown us a new type of love, one that differs from our worldly definition of the word. So how can you and your family participate in that, now and throughout the rest of the year? There are two main ways: prayer and hospitality. Today, we'll talk about prayer.

Does it surprise you that one of the great acts of love we can extend to those around us is prayer? You might have expected something that feels more tangible or that guarantees quicker results, but committed, focused prayerfulness is one of the greatest acts of love you can offer.

When we want to demonstrate our love for someone, we are usually quick to offer plans and solutions. And while those things aren't bad, we skip a step when we don't start by fervently pleading with the Lord on their behalf. When we want to love someone with the kind of love we've seen in Christ, we should first ask God to act in ways that only He can on behalf of them and their circumstances—something even our best laid plans could never do.

Does praying this way feel daunting or overwhelming? For many, the answer is yes, but prayer is simply talking to God. He has not asked us for eloquent speeches or words of grandeur—He simply wants an open channel of communication. The Christmas season presents opportunities to love others—everyone from family to strangers. So when you encounter one of these opportunities, try something different this year—start first with earnest prayer. You might be surprised by the way this grows your love for that person or situation, and what might come of that. Grow in your trust that taking things first to the Lord will yield far better results than you could ever imagine.

Family Time

Talk about these questions with your family or group.

KIDS

1. Why do we pray?

2. Can you think of a prayer you prayed that God has answered clearly? Share that with your family!

TEENS AND ADULTS

3. Why is prayer a better first step than taking action or giving advice?

4. Are there situations in your life where you have been quick to take action but slow to take things to God in prayer? What are some practical ways you can begin to change this habit?

5. Do you believe that God hears and answers your prayers? Why is this sometimes difficult to believe?

Pray

Pray that you would encounter clear opportunities to love others through prayer. Thank God that He has made a way for us to talk to Him, and that He wants to talk with us.

DECEMBER 21

LOVE

Read 1 Peter 4:7-11.

Yesterday we talked about how we can imitate the love of Jesus through prayer. Today we'll look at a second way to do this—by practicing hospitality. What do you associate with that word? The hospitality committee at your church—always prepared with donuts and coffee? Maybe that person whose house is immaculate, who seems to always have fresh cookies on the table, and who is ready to host any one at any time. These are examples of hospitality, but they are not the only ways to demonstrate biblical hospitality.

Biblical hospitality is presence. We see examples of this type of hospitality throughout the Bible. Starting in Genesis, God is hospitable as He creates a garden for His people, full of everything they needed, including His presence. Then we see the tabernacle—a place for Him to dwell in the midst of His people. We see it in the temple in Jerusalem, which is flooded with His presence. And during Advent, we're reminded of His hospitality—His presence—as He put on flesh to dwell among us. And when He left the earth, He did not leave us without Himself. Instead, He gave us the Spirit of God, who now dwells inside of us, forever.

Since we have received this type of hospitality, we now extend it to those around us. We ought to fill our dinner tables with those who do not yet know Him, ministering to those who are lost or broken, not most often with our words but with our presence. Our lives, as believers, should be marked by relationships that call us out of our comfort and into biblical presence and hospitality—a form of ministry we can only pour out because we have first received it.

Consider who among you may be in desperate need of this ministry of presence. Invite those people into your home or to sit with you and your friends at the lunch table. Or simply sit with someone in their joy or sorrow. Take the first steps toward loving others by welcoming others into the hospitality you have received through Christ Jesus.

Family Time

Talk about these questions with your family or group.

KIDS

1. What is one thing you learned this week about Jesus, the Bible, or love?

2. Can you think of any kids at your school or on your sports teams who might sometimes feel left out? What could you do to include them?

TEENS AND ADULTS

3. Think about the examples of God's hospitality from today's devotional. How does God's presence change throughout the Bible? How does it remain the same?

4. Think of a time where this type of "ministry of presence" was impactful for you. What was going on? Why was hospitality more valuable than words in those moments?

5. Why do you struggle to practice hospitality? What feels like a barrier to opening your home or showing hospitality in another way?

Pray

Pray that you would be aware of the hospitality you have received from God, and willing now to extend that to others. Pray, specifically, that He would bring at least one person to mind who you can invite into your life and home this Advent season.

ADVENT

WEEK 4

JOY

DECEMBER 22

JOY

Watch

In the last video of our study, Matt and Lauren talk about joy. What is the difference between happiness and joy, and what does that mean for us as we near closer and closer to Christmas Day?

Watch Video 4 and discuss the questions on the following page with your family or group. See page 5 for instructions on using the QR code.

Scripture

May the God of hope fill you with all joy and peace in believing, so that by the power of the Holy Spirit you may abound in hope.

ROMANS 15:13

Family Time

Talk about these questions with your family or group.

KIDS

1. What makes you joyful at Christmastime?

2. Can you think of a time when you were really excited about something, but in the end it didn't turn out like you thought? What was that like?

TEENS AND ADULTS

3. What do you think is the difference between joy and happiness?

4. Why does Christmas spark a different kind of joy for believers in Christ than for those who don't know Him?

5. Where have you sought to find your identity in things that are fragile, rather than in Christ?

Pray

Pray that as Christmas Day approaches, you will not be distracted from why we are celebrating. Pray that throughout this week, your heart and mind will be focused on the joy you have because of the coming of Christ.

DECEMBER 23

JOY

Read John 15:1-11.

There's a feeling common to most of us; it usually comes on in late afternoon or early evening Christmas Day. After all the presents have been opened and the food has been eaten, you look around at the remnants of Christmas morning and a sense of sadness begins to creep in. All the buildup over the last month—the decorations, the music, the parties, the shopping—has led to this moment, and now it's over. Christmas melodies fade into post-Christmas melancholy.

We end the day feeling this way because in our hearts, we know there is more. We are left wanting. The happiness we experienced surrounding the celebration isn't enough. See, happiness is built upon the things around you—it is fragile and it cannot last. But real joy is something different. It is a deep-rooted gladness that remains regardless of circumstances. It is the feeling of safety and security that comes only through great union with Jesus. It has to be fought for, but it is worth it. Joy outlasts pain and hard circumstances, and it certainly outlasts the disappointment you may feel as you near the end of Christmas Day.

In His coming, Christ brought about this kind of lasting joy. Through His life, death, and resurrection, we have something much less fragile than fleeting feelings of happiness. We have Him, and in Him we have all that we need. He has given us a new identity, His full acceptance and approval, and freedom to walk confidently knowing we are cared for and loved.

When we put our hope in the right place and receive the love of Christ—the Savior whose birth we are so close to celebrating in just two days—we get to then walk out in joy, and that is far better than the fleeting happiness our world has to offer.

Family Time

Talk about these questions with your family or group.

KIDS

1. What are you most excited about for Christmas Day?

2. What does the day after Christmas usually feel like?

TEENS AND ADULTS

3. Why does worldly happiness never last? How have you experienced the lasting joy that comes from Jesus in your life?

4. Is there a situation in your life right now where you need to fight for joy? Why is it tempting to settle for less?

5. Have you found your identity or purpose in fragile, fleeting, worldly things? In what areas of your life would true joy in Christ change things?

Pray

Thank God for the joy we have because of Jesus' life, death, and resurrection. Pray that it would be clear to you where you have settled for worldly happiness instead of joy. Pray God would give you ways to share the joy you have in Christ with others as Christmas approaches.

DECEMBER 24

JOY

Read John 16:16-24.

Joy to the world! the Lord is come; Let earth receive her King;
Let every heart prepare him room, And heaven and nature sing

Take a minute to start this session a little differently. By yourself, with your family, or with your group, listen to "Joy to the World." You may be tempted to skip this part, since you've likely heard this song upwards of hundreds of times ... but slow down, close your eyes, and really listen to the words.

This song does two things—both of which are really simple, yet each should stir up great affection in you for our coming King. First, it gives us reason upon reason why Jesus coming to earth brought great joy for each of us and for the whole world. He has come to rule and reign, with truth and grace. He has come to defeat sin, shame, and death. He has come so that we might see His goodness and righteousness spread through every tribe, tongue, and nation!

The second thing this song does is it calls us to enter into and share the good news of this joy. Over and over the lyrics tell listeners and singers to "repeat the sounding joy." Christmas provides great temptation to lose our focus—to narrow our attention to selfish worldly things, but this song ought to snap us out of that daze and into great affection for the baby who brought true joy into our world. We know the reason tomorrow matters, and we would be fools to keep that to ourselves.

As you prepare for tomorrow, remember why it is that we have such deep joy. Think about this on a global scale, but spend time reflecting on your own life. Where has He brought you out of darkness and into joy? How did His coming change your life? Throughout the day, refocus your heart and your mind on Him. Steal a few moments away from the excitement and chaos to spend time rejoicing in prayer. Spend time with your family and friends, have fun, but do not miss this opportunity to experience and celebrate the arrival of true joy.

Family Time

Talk about these questions with your family or group.

KIDS

1. What is your favorite Christmas carol to sing?

2. What is your favorite part of the song "Joy to the World"? Why?

TEENS AND ADULTS

3. What are some ways you can slow down and refocus your heart and mind on the real reason for celebration tomorrow?

4. How did Jesus' coming to earth change your life? Think of a moment where He brought you out of what felt like inescapable darkness and into everlasting joy. Share if you are comfortable.

5. Who in your life needs to hear the "good news of great joy" of Jesus' coming? What is a tangible step you can take toward sharing that truth with them this Christmas?

Pray

Thank God for sending true joy into the world and for an opportunity to celebrate that tomorrow. Pray for space and time to reflect on why this matters for you. Pray for opportunities to share this joy with the people who might not yet truly understand it.

DECEMBER 25

JOY

Read Luke 2:1-20.

Merry Christmas! We have been preparing our hearts and minds over the last few weeks to celebrate this day rightly, and it is finally here. Today, we celebrate the coming of hope, peace, love, and joy.

We've spent time meditating on the hope that came with His arrival—hope for the Israelites, after waiting hundreds of years for their promised Savior, and hope for us now. We talked about peace—the reminders given to Mary and the shepherds not to be afraid. The good news of Jesus has brought a peace to the world that was previously unimaginable. He also brought with Him love. In fact, He didn't just bring love, He embodied it. He has given us a new example of love—one we can now receive and then imitate through prayer and hospitality. And this week, we've moved toward this day of celebration by talking about joy. Oh, what joy we have in Christ Jesus! Joy that outlasts worldly happiness, and instead roots us in deep and assured gladness.

We have much to celebrate today, but what's next? Though the festivities will end and the decorations will be put away, He should continue to be the focal point of our attention. During these last 25 days, we have marked Christ's first advent—His first coming. But now, we shift our focus to His second advent—when He fulfills His promise to one day come again!

"I am going to show you a secret, John," Jesus said, "about when I come back. Write down what you see so God's children can read it, and wait with happy excitement. I'm on my way...I'll be there soon."[4]

JESUS STORYBOOK BIBLE

Jesus is coming back. We don't know when, but He is coming. Soon we will worship our King forever in the ways He deserves. And so we pray—come, Lord Jesus, come!

Family Time

Talk about these questions with your family or group.

KIDS

1. What is one thing you learned during the last month?

2. How can we remember the joy we have in Jesus today? How can we look forward to the exciting day when Jesus returns?

TEENS AND ADULTS

3. What is one thing you can do to tell or show others about the things you've learned during Advent?

4. How can you "wait well" for Jesus' return?

5. How can you, your family, or group stay focused on hope, peace, love, and joy throughout the entire year?

Pray

Thank God that He sent His Son to be born as a baby, live a perfect life, die for our sins, and be resurrected. Pray that today would not only be a memorable celebration with friends and family, but a day to remember how Jesus' birth changed the world forever. Pray that you would not lose focus, and you would wait well for His return.

FAMILY ACTIVITIES

WEEK I
HOPE

FAMILY ACTIVITY

Make plans for a fun Christmas activity next week that you know your children will love. Perhaps it's seeing a Christmas play or movie, decorating cookies together, or seeing Christmas lights. At the end of your family Advent time, promise your kids that you are going to do something special together to celebrate Advent—something they will love—but don't tell them what or when. As the days go by, remind them of your promise and give them hints as to what it might be. Let their expectation and excitement grow throughout the week. Use this opportunity to remind them of God's promise to send a Rescuer and the anticipation God's people felt as they waited.

COME, THOU LONG-EXPECTED JESUS
Charles Wesley

As a family, sing or listen to "Come, Thou Long-Expected Jesus." As you do, read carefully through the lyrics and explain any words that might be unfamiliar to your kids. Ask them what they learn about Jesus from this song.

Come, Thou long-expected Jesus,
Born to set Thy people free;
From our fears and sins release us,
Let us find our rest in Thee.
Israel's Strength and Consolation,
Hope of all the earth Thou art;
Dear Desire of every nation,
Joy of every longing heart.

Born Thy people to deliver,
Born a child and yet a King,
Born to reign in us forever,
Now Thy gracious kingdom bring.
By Thine own eternal Spirit
Rule in all our hearts alone;
By Thine all sufficient merit,
Raise us to Thy glorious throne.

ADDITIONAL ACTIVITIES

1. Create an Advent wreath to use throughout the Advent season.
2. Create a nativity scene to use throughout the Advent season. If you would like to make this activity last the entire season, consider creating just the stable, animals, and Mary and Joseph this week.
3. Consider a way your family can serve in the community during the Advent season. Here are a few ideas:
   a. Choose a child or family you can provide Christmas gifts to this year. Shop for them together and deliver the gift(s) appropriately.
   b. Visit an elderly care center and sing carols for the residents.
   c. Take dinner to someone you know who is lonely or in need.

WEEK 2
PEACE

FAMILY ACTIVITY

This week, keep the promise you made to your family during last week's family Advent time. Talk about how you fulfilled the hints and clues you gave them. Discuss the experience of waiting: What was it like to wait? What was it like to finally experience what you had been waiting and hoping for? Remember together God's faithfulness in sending a Savior. It happened just as He said it would.

AWAY IN A MANGER
Anonymous

As a family, sing or listen to "Away in a Manger." As you do, read carefully through the lyrics and explain any words that might be unfamiliar to your kids. Ask them what they learn about Jesus from this song.

*Away in a manger,
no crib for a bed,
The little Lord Jesus laid
down His sweet head.*

*The stars in the sky looked
down where He lay,
The little Lord Jesus,
asleep on the hay.*

ADDITIONAL ACTIVITIES

1. Continue making your nativity set. This week, create the baby Jesus piece and add it to the set.
2. Spend time imagining what the "glory of the Lord" shining down on the shepherds was like. Draw what you think it looked like, or turn off the lights and recreate it with flashlights, candles, props, and singing!
3. Draw or paint what you think the night sky might have looked like when the angels appeared to the shepherds.
4. When you see Christmas lights, talk about which lights and houses are your favorites and why. We are attracted to lights because we are made for the Light. Talk with your children about how these lights remind us of Jesus, the best and perfect Light of the world.

WEEK 3
LOVE

FAMILY ACTIVITY

One night this week, go out caroling as a family. As you visit homes of neighbors, friends, and family, sing songs of praise about the birth and salvation of Jesus. It might be easiest to start at the home of someone you know who loves Jesus as you do. Sing praises to God and invite them to join you at the next house.

Make sure you visit at least one home of people who might not love and trust Jesus. Just like God showed grace and love to the lowliest of sinners, share the good news of Jesus' birth with someone who does not know God. Maybe that person will hear the good news and will believe in Jesus.

HARK! THE HERALD ANGELS SING
Charles Wesley

As a family, sing or listen to "Hark! The Herald Angels Sing." As you do, read carefully through the lyrics and explain any words that might be unfamiliar to your kids. Ask them what they learn about Jesus from this song.

Hark! the herald angels sing,
"Glory to the newborn King!"
Peace on earth, and mercy mild,
God and sinners reconciled
Joyful, all ye nations, rise,

Join the triumph of the skies;
With th' angelic host proclaim,
"Christ is born in Bethlehem."
Hark! the herald angels sing,
"Glory to the newborn King!"

ADDITIONAL ACTIVITIES

1. Continue making your nativity set. This week, create shepherds and angel pieces and add them to the set.
2. Use a sock and stuffing to create a baby Jesus doll, wrapped in fabric scraps. Make a manger for the doll out of a paper sack. Let your kids care for baby Jesus and have them use it to retell Jesus' birth story throughout the week.
3. Make a Christmas card for someone who does not love and trust Jesus. Wish them a merry Christmas and tell them that Jesus showed His love on the cross as He came to save sinners!
4. Play hide-and-seek and talk about how Jesus came to seek and save the lost. Thank God for sending Jesus.

WEEK 4
JOY

FAMILY ACTIVITY

TO CELEBRATE JESUS' BIRTH: Plan to have a birthday party for Jesus on Christmas Day! Spend time as a whole family gathering ingredients, making a cake, and decorating it. As you do so, remind your family that we have a reason to celebrate. God promised a Savior and sent us Jesus, the hope of the world!

TO TALK ABOUT JESUS' RETURN: Read 1 Thessalonians 4:13–18 and talk about what Jesus' return will be like, look like, and sound like. What do you learn from this passage? Ask your children what questions they have about Jesus' return and if it's something that scares them to think about. Assure them that Jesus' return will usher in a world with no more sin, sickness, sadness, fights, punishment, or scary storms at bedtime. Even better, those who love and trust Jesus will be with Him forever with no separation. We should look to and long for Jesus' return. And while we wait, we should take seriously His command to love Him first and most, know His Word, care for the poor, and share the gospel.

SILENT NIGHT! HOLY NIGHT!
Joseph Mohr

Sing or listen to "Silent Night" together. As you do, read carefully through the lyrics and explain any words that might be unfamiliar to your kids. Ask them what they learn about Jesus from this song.

Silent night, holy night
All is calm, all is bright
'Round yon virgin mother and child!
Holy infant, so tender and mild,
Sleep in heavenly peace,
Sleep in heavenly peace.

Silent night! Holy night!
Shepherds quake at the sight.
Glories stream from heaven afar,
Heav'nly hosts sing "Alleluia!
Christ the Savior is born!
Christ the Savior is born!"

Silent night! Holy night!
Son of God, love's pure light
Radiant beams from Thy holy face
With the dawn of redeeming grace,
Jesus, Lord at Thy birth!
Jesus, Lord at Thy birth!

Silent night! Holy night!
Wondrous star lend thy light;
With the angels let us sing
"Alleluia" to our King;
"Christ the Savior is born!
Christ the Savior is born!"

FAMILY ACTIVITIES

ADDITIONAL ACTIVITIES

1. Draw or paint what you think Jesus' return might look like.
2. Spend time outside watching the clouds. After Jesus died and came back to life, He returned to heaven by going up into the clouds. The Bible tells us He will return, coming out of the clouds. Spend time imagining what Jesus' return will look like and pray for Him to come soon.

CELEBRATING A NEW FAMILY MEMBER

If another person joined your family this year, there is much to celebrate. Families grow through the birth or adoption of a child, marriage, or taking in a person who needs love and support. Often, when a new person joins a family, they do not have many Christmas ornaments to add to the family tree. Make or purchase a special ornament for your new family member to recognize and remember God's goodness to bring you together.

FIRST CHRISTMAS WITHOUT A FAMILY MEMBER

Celebrating can be hard when your family is grieving the loss of a loved one. Take time to help your child remember and talk about that special person if they need to. Help them to remember the good times and memories they have about that person. If your loved one was a believer, talk about the beautiful reality that they are now with Jesus. Hang an ornament or put out a special decoration that reminds your family of that person. Be honest with God about your sadness and ask Him to make your hearts joyful again.

1. Sally Lloyd-Jones, The Jesus Storybook Bible: Every Story Whispers His Name (Grand Rapids, MI: Zonderkidz, 2007), p. 35.
2. Oxford Lanauges Dictionary (accessed via https://languages.oup.com/dictionaries/)
3. C. S. Lewis, The Four Loves (New York, NY: Harcourt Brace, 1960).
4. Lloyd-Jones, p. 342, 348.

'Twas the night before Christmas...

It's hard to find a human being who isn't moved or captivated by a good story. This is because we are created to live in a story—the Christian story.

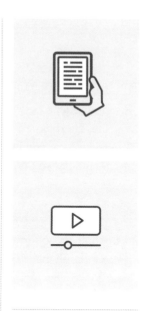

People are both drawn to stories and shaped by stories. But given our bent toward sin, away from the one true story, we often find ourselves caught up in the false stories of our culture.

Amid the chaos and busyness of everyday life, we buy into false narratives such as consumerism, secularism, nationalism, progressivism, and cynicism. Though we may not confess these stories to be true with our mouths, we act as if they are true with our lives.

During Advent, we can press into the story of Jesus' birth and allow it to reorient our hearts and minds toward Christ. This 25-day devotional experience can help you:

- Enrich yourself (and your family) spiritually by immersing in the Advent season.
- Grow in spiritual maturity with optional family or group discipleship activities.
- Gain a greater appreciation of a broad Christian tradition.
- Anticipate the second coming of Jesus.
- Develop new Christmas traditions.

ADDITIONAL RESOURCES

FAMILY ADVENT DEVOTIONAL eBOOK
The eBook includes the content of this printed book but offers the convenience and flexibility that come with mobile technology.

eBook
005834614 $12.99

VIDEO CONTENT
Four free streamable videos featuring Matt and Lauren Chandler are available at lifeway.com/familyadventvideos

Price and availability subject to change without notice.